# SMALL TALK COURSE FOR (PROSPECTIVE) NETWORKERS

EXPAND YOUR NETWORK MONTHLY BY MORE THAN 100 NEW PEOPLE AND WIN A SOLID FOUNDATION FOR BUILDING YOUR BUSINESS.

DANIEL KERN

Copyright © Daniel Kern
All Rights Reserved.

ISBN 978-1-63957-071-3

This book has been published with all efforts taken to make the material error-free after the consent of the author. However, the author and the publisher do not assume and hereby disclaim any liability to any party for any loss, damage, or disruption caused by errors or omissions, whether such errors or omissions result from negligence, accident, or any other cause.

While every effort has been made to avoid any mistake or omission, this publication is being sold on the condition and understanding that neither the author nor the publishers or printers would be liable in any manner to any person by reason of any mistake or omission in this publication or for any action taken or omitted to be taken or advice rendered or accepted on the basis of this work. For any defect in printing or binding the publishers will be liable only to replace the defective copy by another copy of this work then available.

# Contents

*Preface* — v

1. Small Talk – What Is It? — 1
2. Training To Become A Professional Small Talker — 3
3. The Four Phases Of Small Talk — 5
4. Goals Make The Difference — 18
5. Possible Mistakes During Small Talk — 20
6. Subsequent Work — 22
7. The Training Program — 23
8. 3 – 2 – 1 – Start! — 25

Disclaimer — 27

# Preface

Dear reader,

Have you ever watched young children as they approach one another? If they encounter a new, unknown child, they approach each other with curiosity. They simply start talking and then they start playing with each other. They do not fear that the other one might reject them. That is the way our children win new friends.

Many adults find approaching others much more difficult. Just the idea of approaching a total stranger causes them anxiety. Immediately, there arise thousands and thousands of questions in their head: »What if the person finds my approach pushy? Maybe I say something stupid or disturb the person...« Within a short time, we convince ourselves that it is in everyone's interest to leave the person alone. And that is exactly what we do.

This book will provide you with a new strategy. To be precise, what you will learn with this book is not even new to you. Most likely you also had no problems with approaching unknown children (and also adults) in your early childhood. In this sense, this book should help you to free a submerged ability so that you are again able to meet and get to know complete strangers with interest.

Even though the examples from this book are from a business context, you can equally use the provided skills to enlarge your private network, to expand your circle of friends and even to find a life partner.

In whatever way you will use your new skills, I wish you every success with it!

Yours, Daniel Kern

CHAPTER ONE

# Small talk – what is it?

Wikipedia writes about small talk:

- *A casual conversation without a lot of depth is considered small talk.*
- *Although the topics are insignificant and interchangeable, small talk as a social ritual has great significance. It avoids awkward silence, loosens the atmosphere and is the start of getting to know others, for example, business partners. Small talk indicates the interest in the other person or at least feigns it. The topics among strangers are usually very general. Almost literally is the term "talking about the weather". This topic has the advantage that everyone can have an opinion about it and that differences in opinion are acceptable. Furthermore, the weather can have an influence on the activities of a person and thus lead to other, more personal topics.*
- *Typical questions are for example:*
- *„How are you?" (as an introduction)*
- *„How is your family?" (among adults)*
- *„What are you doing today?" (to get to a topic that is wider)*
- *Sometimes even the fact that one needs to "tell" something leads to small talk. Moreover, if one casually wants to know something specific, small talk can be used as a means to*

*broach a subject inconspicuously. A good way to change the subject is to ask questions.*
- *People who are more often involved in small talk than in profound discussions are supposed to be happier according to scientific studies.*
- *If one is more familiar with someone, it is free to choose whether to start a conversation with small talk or to start with a specific topic immediately.*

Small talk is about getting into a conversation with somebody and about approaching each other verbally. Mutually both partners find out whether they want to intensify the conversation or just want to have a nice little conversation to pass the time.

CHAPTER TWO

# Training to become a professional small talker

Small talk training includes two main topics. The first part shows how you can overcome your own contact anxiety so that you are able to approach other people just like in your childhood and simply say »hello«.

If you are among the group of people that finds it hard to approach strangers, you belong to the great majority.

I admit that I myself was a contact grouch for a long time. If there was a bar table at a business party where there was no danger of someone else joining, I stood exactly there. After some hours of »networking« I left the party frustrated and got annoyed about myself for having wasted yet another evening and for having paid way too much for entry and food.

Even today, it still happens that tons and tons of counter-arguments arise in my head when I think about addressing a stranger. Almost everyone knows that. On some days, I give in to these objections. If I overcome them and approach people, in almost all cases, a boring event becomes an exciting party with many interesting people and conversations - and often one contact or another becomes a business partner.

Eventually, I had been to what felt like thousand networking events, where I stood around and enviously watched others communicating with one another, having fun, arranging meetings or exchanging contact information. My only profit from participating in this event were a few morsels from the buffet and one or two drinks.

It could not go on like this and I decided to work on myself. But the way I am: The whole thing had to be planned and that is how I developed my own small talk training course. This is the base of what you are reading here. However, you may have guessed it: One should not let someone else who knows nothing about the subject develop a training course. That must go wrong.

In fact, it did; at least at the beginning, I made many mistakes. For this reason, I will not publish the original plan here, but rather what has become of it - the result of my own development; what I have learned from my successes and failures.

That the whole thing is successful can be noticed when taking into account that the majority of my sales and earnings is made up of business with people from my network or recommendations to their friends.

CHAPTER THREE

# The four phases of small talk

I have developed the four-phase model myself. Especially a topic that is for many people associated with feelings, such as discomfort and anxiety, should be divided into smaller, more structured and more manageable units.

The four-phase model consists of the logical steps of small talk.

## *Phase 1: Getting into conversation*

The first step is about approaching a person. It is exactly this procedure that causes most people quite a headache. Many fear rejection. What if the other person finds me annoying, if I embarrass myself, if I make a mistake or if the other person does not speak my language? We feel vulnerable in this situation. We reveal our wish to get to know the other person and are afraid of getting rejected.

With this everyone has his own techniques. I myself tend to overdraw the situation and to picture its most extreme outcome. Perhaps I am dealing with a crazy serial killer that wants to prepare my innards as a delicacy just like Hannibal Lecter. At the latest when I imagine my interlocutor wearing the mask of Hannibal Lecter from the movie, I have overcome my fears and have to smile. But honest smiling and fear are mutually exclusive. Others make sure that they are aware of the fact that they are well prepared and that they have prepared many interesting topics that are suitable for starting a conversation.

Before starting the actual conversation, look at the person you want to address for a short time. Do you find some positive and interesting aspects on him (or her)? This will help you to approach the person with a positive attitude. People unconsciously notice how people relate to them and with positive thoughts towards them you can make the approach considerably easier.

Research has found out that only 5 to 7 percent of communication consist of words. 35 to 38 percent we get from nonverbal communication. That means the way we approach others, including countenance and gesture, our stress and relaxation, etc. If you took the time in advance to bring someone else a positive feeling, it would dramatically improve the elements of the nonverbal communication which we can hardly influence consciously.

Then in your thought, you go over your list of topics and think about what topic would be particularly suitable for addressing the person. Depending on the situation and your feelings, how you perceived the situation, you can decide whether you want to choose one of the topics you prepared (which are, so to say, the safety topics if nothing else comes to your mind) or whether the situation brings up a topic that fits more.

When starting the conversation do not forget to shortly introduce yourself. Depending on the circumstances and the customs of the group this can mean saying your first name, first name and surname or anything alike. If you are new in this group, look at how the others proceed.

For the actual speech, an open question is suitable because the interlocutor can simply find an answer to that. What is meant is a question which one cannot just be answered with yes or no, but a question that leads to a longer answer. Within a professional context, a question regarding their occupation seems to make sense.

Small talk is not so much about telling others something, but rather about talking in order to start a conversation with someone. To accomplish that, it is best to encourage the other person to talk. Much scientific research has shown that people perceive others as positive and interesting if they listen to them.

Of course, the whole thing should not end as an interrogation and you should also try to involve yourself. We tend to say more than usual when we are in a situation in which we feel insecure.

Charisma and body language

According to scientific insights, our body language influences more than 50 percent of our communication. This way the person that talks to us perceives very quickly if what we say with words corresponds to reality.

Do you know the saying that there is no second chance for a first impression? And especially the first impression consists to a large extent of our body language. Besides appearance and clothes, also posture, charisma and gestures contribute to the first impression. The person opposite perceives all of this information before we even have expressed a single word.

Body language and charisma are levels of communication on which we can only deliberately operate to a limited extent. If you approach someone in order to talk to them and you already feel as if the they refused any contact, you will radiate that exact expectation. You will approach your interlocutor like an intimidated child or like a kicked dog.

Is this the way you want to come across? Do you think that you will appeal to you interlocutor this way? Then do something against it. Rather than thinking about what could go wrong, ask yourself what would be the best that could happen. Imagine the whole thing vividly. The person opposite could become your best friend, your business or life partner. Imagine that you have already achieved that.

Think of conversational situations from your past where conversations proceeded positively and brought the desired results. If you have a positive idea, start to smile. The movement of your facial muscles while smiling causes a release of endorphins. With doing this, you will automatically feel better and you will also radiate that.

Another aspect is body language. Avoid crossing your arms, clenching your fists or putting your hands into your pockets. Be modest with your gestures and stand as still as possible. The former implies a rejection of the other person and the latter implies nervousness. If you do not know what to do with your hands, hold a drink or your purse.

Search eye contact and entirely concentrate on your interlocutor. With doing this, you give the other person the impression that you listen to him. In a conversation try to not only consider the words, but also the facial expressions and gestures of the person opposite (this perhaps needs a bit of practice, but will help you to perceive your interlocutor more).

If are more experienced with small talk, you can start to carefully and cleverly copy the facial expressions, gestures, speaking rate, word choice, intonation, etc. of your interlocutor. In NLP[1] one talks of »pacing« in this context.

Finding topics

The second part of the preparation phase is about thinking of topics so that you can build up a casual conversation together with your interlocutor. Such topics must meet some criteria.

Criteria for the topics:

- positive topics
- appreciate topics
- no controversial topics (nothing that leads to a »dispute«)
- nothing TOO personal
- nothing that could hurt the other person
- no politics, no religion, no sex

With small talk, your first goal is to get talking to somebody. It is, therefore, important to choose topics, but also contributions to the conversation that make the person feel »comfortable«. In this phase of the conversation the persons concerned make first contact and slightly get to know each other. With this, positive topics are important and also topics that make the interlocutor feel positive. It is not the goal to start small talk with »the big problems of the world« unless you are at an event where this is »the topic«.

Also, make sure to comment on your fellow human beings in an appreciative way. You do not know your interlocutor's attitude towards the persons concerned; moreover, your interlocutor will ask himself what you will say about himself after the conversation is over.

At the earliest if you have built a solid conversational foundation politics, religion, sex and controversial topics of all kinds can be addressed. You should also avoid mentioning too personal issues. You have not yet bonded with the other one. People that immediately talk about their life story, all of their anxieties, worries, infirmities and illnesses, can easily overwhelm their interlocutor. When choosing topics, always make sure that the other person can actually contribute something to the conversation. If you are not on a chemist congress, you should not discuss the topic that was awarded the latest Nobel Prize in Chemistry.

Topics that I like to use for the first phase of conversation:

**Things that I like / enjoy:** Some examples that are suitable are special pieces of music, beautiful views, the nice weather, new movies ...

**Interests:** The other person might find your personal interests interesting, but be modest. The aim is to start a conversation and no to make a speech.

**Current issues:** You can mention current issues unless they are too controversial. The official visit of the queen is acceptable, computer prediction of elections not so much.

**Personal news:** Of course you can tell that you have become a mother last week or that your son has recently passed his second state examination. The lovesickness of your daughter or that your wife invited you to a couple counseling are not very suitable as conversation starters.

**Sports:** Almost everyone can say something about sports.

**Hobbies and leisure time activities:** Especially, if you discover common interests, hobbies provide an almost infinite amount of topics for conversation. The same goes for music, movies, books, TV shows, cars ...

**A story:** If you have experienced something funny, interesting, odd or surprising, this experience can be a good conversation starter as long as the mentioned limitations are considered.

**Event topics**: The current event or location you are at is also suitable as a topic. Again, you should not hurt anybody. You do not know what your interlocutor thinks of the event organizer or the current topic.

**Questions**: An easy way of starting a conversation is to ask the other person something, e.g. regarding the event program or how the person found the last speech.

**Everyday topics**: Also uncritical conversation starters are: the weather, the location where you are at or special features of your environment.

I have a whole list of such topics on which I continuously work. Some topics are out by now, new ones are added.

Of course, this is not about always bringing the list with you so that you can look on it if necessary. And even if you do not hold all the topics in your head: If your list comprises 20, 30 or 40 topics, you will remember some if necessary.

Examples for starting a conversation

Here are some conversation starters that have worked for me. Just as some people are different from others, conversation starters also vary. It makes sense to develop your own instead of just copying other's. Look at the following as inspiration for developing own ones. I usually start with »hello, my name is X ...« Depending on my environment, a casual »hello« can become a »good evening« or something similar.

My openers:

- How long do you know the host? / Where do you know him from?

- Are you also from the branch XY? (depending on the event)
- I found the topic of the lecture interesting. Do you have experience with the topic?
- The weather today is ..., Don't you agree?
- What do you think of the food? Can you recommend something?
- I really like your shoes. Where can I buy them?
- Have you been working for X for a long time already?
- Do you take this train more often?
- How was your arrival?
- Did you also have troubles finding a parking spot?
- What does your company do?
- Can you tell me where I can buy something to drink?
- What do you think of the XY game on the weekend?
- Have you also been stuck in the traffic jam?

As you can see: Not every topic and every question is suitable. Over time, you will get a feel for what is acceptable and what leads to further conversation.

Approaching an existent group

Especially, if you are »the new one« in an already existing group, an existing club or an existing organization, it can be difficult to start a conversation. Many people tend to debase themselves in a situation like this in order to not attract attention as »the new one«. This additionally reduces the probability of being addressed.

At an event where apparently everyone already knows each other and chats with one another, the easiest way is to just join a group of talking people. Frankly, say that you do not know anybody, yet, and you would like to join. You will hardly be met with refusal and can contribute to the conversation.

Now it is vital to interestedly follow the conversation and to actively contribute to it, for example, with a query. If you cannot do that, wait until the conversation slowly calms down; then try to steer it in a direction that suits you more. In this context »who asks also leads« applies, too. Questions indicate that you are interested and increase the willingness of the other person to listen to you and show interest in your statements and questions as well.

## *Phase 2: Continuing the conversation*

With a little practice, you will find it increasingly easier to have stimulating conversations with people. Two approaches are going to be described below. What is important here is to listen to your interlocutor carefully. It will give you the opportunity to plan the continuation of the conversation.

Realizing conversation offers

Do you know this conversational situation? You pluck up the courage to approach a person. Then this person's responds, for example:

» I am sorry, I do not know my way around here. I moved here only a few days ago because I will start a new job next week.«

As an inexperienced small talker, you will maybe realize that this answer makes all of your other topics from your list useless. Your carefully planned framework collapses like a house of cards. However, if you are an experienced small talker, you will recognize that the answer offers several other topics. Examples could be:

Where are you from?

Which job are you going to start?

I myself have moved several times. How did you get through all of the stress from moving?

...

Although the skill is called »small talk«. The actual core competence is listening. I you listen properly, you will notice that your interlocutor will in most cases make a variety of conversation offers.

Recognizing hot spots

Recognizing hot spots is the ability to know what topics interest and suit your interlocutor by just looking at him. If you have not done your »homework« beforehand and, therefore, have no picture of the person, pay attention to the following points:

- **Clothing**: presumptive price range, neat, age, style, appropriate for the occasion ...
- **Symbols of affiliation**: pins, collar embroidery, special rings, bags or purses with prints or logos
- **Shoes**: price range, neat, age, style
- **Personal appearance**: hair, beard, skin tone, healthy or fragile appearance, approximate age
- **Persons they are talking to at the moment**: Who is the person talking to? (if not known – try to capture what the person is like with the same pattern)
- **Consumption**: Does the person eat, drink or smoke at the moment – what?
- **Posture, charisma**: How does the person act, how do others interact with that person?

Once you have a picture of your interlocutor, some suitable topics will come to your mind and other unsuitable ones can be dropped. A harmless possibility for starting a conversation can be an emblem on the collar or the lapel.

These present wonderful possibilities to ask for the meaning of the emblem. It is also a good idea to use an emblem yourself. If you are a fan of soccer, it can be the emblem of your favorite team or the logo of a team that lies at your heart. Or you purchase something comparable that makes it easier for others to approach you. However, make sure that you avoid using controversial symbols, such as logos of political parties, unless you want to be confronted by somebody because of the logo and want to risk that others might want to avoid you because of the symbol.

## *Phase 3: Intensifying a conversation*

After you have approached each other verbally and once a base for communication is established, both of you will notice if you want to have a more profound conversation. It is alright if you want to stay on the level of superficial chatting. You can also always decide to end the conversation. I will give you some advice on how to do this in phase 4.

The most commonly used possibility to bring a conversation from the level of chatting to a higher one is to reveal something about yourself or to ask the other person a question that demands a more personal answer.

Initially, this will need a bit of courage and of course, one also needs some tact in order to not overwhelm the other person with your statements and questions. But you will notice that this step will make you both bond a little more. Requirement for this step is that you have established a good communicative base during the more superficial exchange.

Now you can also address more controversial topics. If the conversation is based on mutual sympathy, topics like this can be nicely discussed. Your interlocutor is now able to handle an opinion of you that is different from his. He can also feel your openness if he has another opinion. A respectful, appreciative communicative climate and the mutual willingness to accept other opinions are fundament for this.

Examples for questions to bring a conversation on to a more personal level:

- What is important to you in life?
- What are your occupational / personal goals?
- Why did you choose the job XXX / the company YYY?
- Do you have a child or would you like to have children?
- What was your dream job when you were a child?
- What makes you happy?
- What inspires you?
- Where do you see yourself in 10 years?

## *Phase 4: Ending the conversation*

There are different reasons for ending a conversation. One reason could be that everyone in starting to lose interest in the discussion or another reason could be that you notice that your interlocutor is getting restless. As a good conversational partner, you act accordingly.

When you are ending a conversation, it is important that you communicate the reason for that. Therefore, the other person does not get the impression that he said something wrong or that he bored you. This could disrupt the newly initiated contact sustainably.

Always indicate a plausible reason why you have to end the conversation. Thank the person for the conversation and shake your interlocutor's hand. While doing that - if you want to - you can ask the other person for an appointment or his business card in order to continue your conversation at a later time. A smile completes the conversation on a positive note.

CHAPTER FOUR

# Goals make the difference

Many people attend events in order to extend their network. Whether they want to do that in their private or professional life, does not play a big role. Most people only have very limited success with that. Many of them take – provided that it is available – the list of participants home with them and thus have the impression of having achieved something. Others are proud that they talked to four or five people and even got a business card from half of them.

Successful networkers proceed differently. They plan events in advance. Wherever possible, they obtain information on who will attend the event (for example, when events are organized on XING and the list of participants is visible to all guests).

Do that as well. Analyze in advance who the participants are and what could be interesting about them. You can put those who will be of interest to you on your personal to-do list. The self-imposed task for the evening could be to make contact with this person and to get a business card. If one of the persons you wanted to talk to did not come to the event or if you did not have the opportunity to talk, nothing speaks against contacting the person after the event to tell him that you would have liked to talk to him in the evening. Such a call can lead to an appointment for lunch or for the next event.

If you do not have information about the participants in advance, you should at least set yourself quantitative goals: For example, you want to have a conversation with ten new people and get five business cards as well as an appointment for another meeting.

CHAPTER FIVE

# Possible mistakes during small talk

Many people have negative experiences with small talk and can often not say what the mistake was. Of course, there are many sources of error. However, the most common are:

**Questioning:** There is a fine line between interestedly questioning and grilling your interlocutor. While the former signals interest in the person, the latter makes your interlocutor feel as if he were in an interrogation.

**Bragging:** Of course you are allowed to show your positive sides. But those who pretend to be experts for everything, to know everything and every place, etc., will soon seem unsympathetic to the other person. In the case of doubt, it is better to laugh together at a small mistake than to try to impress other people as if you were a »hero«.

**Controversial topics and statement:** Those who try to enter a conversation with controversial topics or provocations and teasing will run the risk of ending up alone.

**Lack of empathy:** Those who seem as if they would not perceive and appreciate their interlocutor will get back the same attitude from the other personconcerned.

**Opening a sales talk:** Again and again, people switch to sales talk after only three sentences of »alibi small talk«. Suddenly, topics, such as retirement security or vital substance supply are elaborated and the person communicates that he is an expert and has to offer a wonderful product. With this, you not only notice an inexperienced small talker, but also an unsuccessful salesman who is under a lot of »pressure«.

**Assertiveness and lack of tolerance:** There are people who want to dominate conversations. With your statements, you make clear that you are right and that you do not accept other opinions. The conversational partner will not feel perceived, rebuked and suppressed and he will end the conversation or continue it on a superficial level.

**You talk too fast, too much and to slurred:** Especially if you feel insecure, you tend to speak slurred, incoherent, too much or too fast. Especially during small talk you have to make sure that you speak clearly and articulately. It is important that the other person understands you well.

CHAPTER SIX

# Subsequent work

If you not just use small talk to pass time, subsequently working on it is also an important part. Develop a file for all the persons you meet. In the electronic age, contact management can also be done with the help of a respective software or an online tool. For this, you fill in all data of the contact that is important to you – but even more to your business partner. Plan appointments for the next meeting. Especially contacts acquired through small talk have a relatively short half-life, in which they have to be reactivated if they are not supposed to be forgotten.

Imagine how your new contact will react if you call him the coming week to ask him how his trip to X went. Or ask your contact to wish his wife a happy birthday from you because after the last conversation you noted that her birthday was on June 17$^{th}$. With this, you start to bond with the person after you have made first contact.

CHAPTER SEVEN

# The training program

Small talk can be learned and trained just like high jump, bicycling or playing an instrument. Take a month's time to sustainably improve your skills and to make small talk into a positive habit.

Your program

Read at least the first three pages of a major newspaper (representing national and international subjects) every day or deliberately watch a daily newscast. News are wonderful small talk topics to which everyone knows something that he can contribute.

Think about five small talk questions to this (or to other topics) that allow you to start a conversation or keep it going.

Talk every day to at least one person and engage in a short conversation with them.

It only counts if the small talk went on for at least five minutes.

If you are using small talk in the business context, then exchange contact information or business cards with at least one person.

Keep a success diary in which you write what worked and what did not work every night. If you did not have enough success, look up what you have done differently on more successful days and try it this way again.

## CHAPTER EIGHT

# 3 – 2 – 1 – start!

Congratulations. Now you know everything you need to become a successful small talker and thus to expand your professional and personal network considerably.

However, please be aware of one thing: What you know does not make you successful - only what you apply takes you further. It is up to you whether you have just read another book and thus passed some time, or if you apply your knowledge actively and successfully.

Again and again, I hear from people that they want to begin to grow as persons after the vacation, after the holidays, after the weekend, next week or next month, when there is less to do.

This, of course, is your decision and I will accept it. But be honest: If you do not start today to approach a person (who may also be on vacation at the beach, on the holiday party, on the Sunday stroll, or in the cafeteria) the likelihood that you will ever do it will virtually be zero.

Only you can decide whether you will become a successful networker with the acquired knowledge.

I wish you every success!
Yours, Daniel Kern

# Disclaimer

**Introduction**

By using this book, you accept this disclaimer in full.

**No advice**

The book contains information. The information is not advice and should not be treated as such.

**No representations or warranties**

To the maximum extent permitted by applicable law and subject to section below, we exclude all representations, warranties, undertakings and guarantees relating to the book.

Without prejudice to the generality of the foregoing paragraph, we do not represent, warrant, undertake or guarantee:

- that the information in the book is correct, accurate, complete or non-misleading.

- that the use of the guidance in the book will lead to any particular outcome or result.

**Limitations and exclusions of liability**

The limitations and exclusions of liability set out in this section and elsewhere in this disclaimer: are subject to section 6 below; and govern all liabilities arising under the disclaimer or in relation to the book, including liabilities arising in contract, in tort (including negligence) and for breach of statutory duty.

We will not be liable to you in respect of any losses arising out of any event or events beyond our reasonable control.

DISCLAIMER

We will not be liable to you in respect of any business losses, including without limitation loss of or damage to profits, income, revenue, use, production, anticipated savings, business, contracts, commercial opportunities or goodwill.

We will not be liable to you in respect of any loss or corruption of any data, database or software.

We will not be liable to you in respect of any special, indirect or consequential loss or damage.

**Exceptions**

Nothing in this disclaimer shall: limit or exclude our liability for death or personal injury resulting from negligence; limit or exclude our liability for fraud or fraudulent misrepresentation; limit any of our liabilities in any way that is not permitted under applicable law; or exclude any of our liabilities that may not be excluded under applicable law.

**Severability**

If a section of this disclaimer is determined by any court or other competent authority to be unlawful and/or unenforceable, the other sections of this disclaimer continue in effect.

If any unlawful and/or unenforceable section would be lawful or enforceable if part of it were deleted, that part will be deemed to be deleted, and the rest of the section will continue in effect.

**Law and jurisdiction**

This disclaimer will be governed by and construed in accordance with Swiss law, and any disputes relating to this disclaimer will be subject to the exclusive jurisdiction of the courts of Switzerland.

www.ingramcontent.com/pod-product-compliance
Lightning Source LLC
Chambersburg PA
CBHW021548200526
45163CB00016B/3089